THE

Modern Reader's Guide

TO

MARK

WILLIAM HAMILTON

ASSOCIATION PRESS · NEW YORK

Contents

THE MODERN READER'S GUIDE

TO MARK

Preface

THE PURPOSE OF THIS "READER'S GUIDE" is simple: to enable the reader to understand intelligently a basic Christian document. I am convinced that lay groups in the churches and students on the campuses are beginning to realize that careful Bible study is one form of Christian obedience that must not be avoided. This guide is meant to be a contribution to that study, without which Protestantism cannot effectively live, think, or act.

By itself, the little book would be useless and unintelligible. The reader will need a copy of The Gospel According to Mark alongside, which can be found in most homes and bookstores. There are many useful and even sprightly books *about* the Bible on the market today. Their function is in general to make us feel that we ought to read the Bible and that we might find it enjoyable. The Bible, however, still presents some problems to the modern reader as he faces the actual text, and so this book tries to meet some of those problems for the person—alone or in a group —who is willing to sit before the material and allow it to speak to him.

There is little that is original in the content of *The Modern Reader's Guide to Mark*. I have drawn heavily on the work of the experts in the field of biblical studies: Frederick C. Grant, A. M. Hunter, C. H. Dodd, Vincent Taylor, and some others. In one sense, the work of the author has been little more than that of an editor, but the form may be slightly more original. This is neither a study guide such as the student movement sometimes uses nor a commentary such as scholars hope that Christian ministers use. It is something in between—fuller and more technical than the first, less technical and more practical than the second—and therefore of more value, I hope, for the layman.

Uniform with this book are two others, from the same author and publisher, which the reader may wish to consult: *The Modern Reader's Guide to Matthew and Luke,* and *The Modern Reader's Guide to John.*

The citations and references to the Bible herein are from the Revised Standard Version of The Holy Bible.

—WILLIAM HAMILTON

THE MODERN READER'S GUIDE

TO MARK

Introduction

IN THE WINTER OF A.D. 64-65 a great fire broke out in Rome, and the emperor Nero looked around for someone to blame. He decided to accuse the Christians who were generally unpopular and were thought to harbor revolutionary ideas. A reign of terror followed; Peter and Paul were probably among the victims.

Shortly after this a little book appeared in Rome bearing the title "The Gospel of Jesus Christ." It was what we know as Mark's gospel, and we can guess at the motives which led to its appearance. Christians under persecution needed to be reminded of their Master and of the sufferings he had undergone. Especially now that the older generation who had known him was dying off, the remembered facts about Jesus needed to be set down.

Let us look at the historical situation at the time. Palestine is under Roman military and civil occupation. A priestly aristocracy (the Sadducees) is chiefly concerned to maintain its own privileged position under the Romans. The religious leaders (the Pharisees) have largely ceased to give an effective lead, and have become more and more absorbed in pious practices at the cost of the "weightier matters of the Law." The common people are neglected and depressed. Political agitators and religious fanatics are preaching violence. There are wild hopes in the air of revolution or of an approaching miraculous deliverance associated with the name of the coming Messiah or Christ. Forty years later, indeed, these pressures were to erupt into a disastrous war which would finish the Jewish state. At the time of which we are speaking, they are brewing.

Into this scene Jesus entered. His answers to the question about the tax to Caesar (12:17) probably bothered the nationalists.

His act of clearing the temple of money-changers upset the priests. His attitude to the Sabbath laws disturbed the pious. Very few understood his association with the people outside the Jewish law—the publicans and sinners. Since he offended nearly everyone, it is not surprising that the Jewish authorities were able to agree to have him put out of the way.

As you read through The Gospel According to Mark, you will note that it is in the form of a series of episodes, loosely strung together. An episode may be told with a good deal of picturesque detail, but then the author is likely to pass on to something else quite abruptly with only a bare summary to show the interconnection. There is little in Mark that can be called continuous biographical narrative.

There is one exception. In Chapters 14 and 15—the so-called Passion story—we find a continuous narrative, telling in detail how Jesus was seized by his enemies, tried, and put to death. At first reading this Passion narrative seems simply to be the story of a good man, denied and deserted by his followers, trapped by religious leaders, condemned by a timid judge, and put to an ignominious death.

A second glance, however, at these critical chapters reveals that there is something more here than a tale of martyrdom. There is a mysterious undercurrent. For example, after the homely details of the preparation of the last supper with the disciples, we read the strange words, "this is my body," "this is my blood . . . poured out for many." The death to come is said to be like a sacrifice, re-establishing a new set of relations between God and man. Again, in the garden of Gethsemane, Jesus says that God wants this execution to take place. Before the high priest, Jesus apparently declares that he is the Messiah, the Son of God, and adds something about the Son of man returning to the right hand of God. Finally, at the end, the "curtain of the temple was torn in two, from top to bottom." This curtain was what hid the presence of God from the people in the Jewish worship, and Mark is apparently suggesting that in the death of Jesus there was something that removed the curtain and made God more accessible. Something deeper and more mysterious is going on, something to do with God's access to men and the deepest issues of human destiny.

Over and over again we hear of a "secret" that must be kept until the right time comes, a secret that seems to have something to do with God's rule over the world. The mystery of the kingdom of God, Mark calls it. It is also the secret of who Jesus really is. Teacher, prophet, reformer, leader? Yes, but what else? The question is put by Jesus himself to his disciples (8:27) in a scene which is evidently intended to be one of the highlights of the picture. The disciples partly understand and partly do not.

Jesus moves throughout this story almost

incognito. He is always something more than appears. But although the actors in the story are barely half aware whom they are dealing with, Mark has already taken his readers into his confidence in the opening verses of the gospel. Here Jesus is contrasted with John the Baptist, here his "secret" is spoken by a divine voice which he alone hears. He is the supernatural Son of God. And soon we stumble upon his works of healing, done with a strange authority. Later we read words, scarcely understood at all by the disciples at the time, about the Son of man having to suffer and die, and be raised again. Who was this man, and what was happening through him? This is *the* question of the gospel, and to it we must now turn.

I. Prologue to Mark's Gospel
1:1-13

1. John the Baptist and his message, 1:1-8

Verse 1 is properly the title of the whole work. The word "Gospel" does not refer to the book itself, or to the words spoken by Jesus. It means the good news of God which is announced through Jesus Christ. Mark speaks of Jesus Christ: Jesus is the Greek form of the Jewish name Joshua; Christ is the Greek equivalent of the Jewish term Messiah, the divine deliverer expected by the Jewish people. At first, Christ was a title; by now it has become part of the proper name.

"Son of God" is perhaps Mark's most significant description of Jesus. It is well to note the decisive places "Son of God" appears in the gospel: here; in the mouths of the demoniacs in 3:11 and 5:7; in the question of the high priest in 14:61; and also in 1:11, 9:7, and

(possibly) 13:32. For Mark, Son of God refers to a divine being that appears in human
form. Mark takes with full seriousness the
reality of the earthly life of Jesus, but for him
this lowly man of suffering is of supernatural
origin. This origin, we shall see, is concealed
from all except those who are prepared to
understand. One of the basic questions of this
gospel lies precisely here: How can one pre-
pare himself to receive this truth? The question is raised in many forms in the New Testament. As Mark phrases it, it is this: How can
one enter the kingdom of God? But when
Paul speaks of salvation or redemption, or
when John tells of the gift of new and eternal
life, it is the same gift of God that is being
described. "Son of God" does not refer to
Jesus as the Messiah; Mark has other ways of
describing this; it is his way of describing
Jesus' utterly unique relationship to God and
His purpose.

John the Baptist is portrayed as one of the
Old Testament prophets, dressed as they

were, preaching a similar message of repentance and forgiveness. The locusts he ate were the insects, not the seeds of the tree. He expresses his humility by declaring himself unfit even to perform the slave's task of untying the sandal of the one who is to come after him.

2. *Jesus' baptism, 1:9-11*

The baptisms that John performed required repentance, yet Jesus submitted himself to this baptism. Did he confess his sin? Mark is not yet aware of this problem, though Matthew 3:14-15 attempts to deal with it. When we try to penetrate behind the imagery, just what event in the career of Jesus is being portrayed? The heavens open: God's access to man is now made direct. A voice from God speaks: Jesus' vocation is defined. (If you look carefully at these words you will see that they are taken from Psalm 2:7 and Isaiah 42:1. Already at the beginning, Jesus' meaning is being defined in terms both of the divine Son of God and of the lowly servant of God.) The Spirit descends: power is given to perform his ministry. This does not mean that because the Spirit descended on Jesus he then became the Son of God. The descent of the Spirit is a sign pointing to the fact that he is already, and has been from the beginning, God's Son.

The "voice" is heard only by Jesus himself. A clear-cut decision has been made about his relation to the kingdom of God.

3. *the temptation, 1:12-13*

Notice the contrast between the very exalted experience of baptism and this description of loneliness and perhaps even terror. The fuller accounts of this in Matthew 4:1-11 and Luke 4:1-13 help us to round out our picture of the meaning of these verses. God drives Jesus to the wilderness, but it is Satan that tempts him.

II. The Ministry in Galilee
1:14—6:13

1. the first phase, 1:14—3:6

Any divisions of the material are always partly arbitrary. Perhaps the best way is to try to organize the material by means of the geography. This first phase finds Jesus mainly in the towns. After 3:6 he goes into the countryside because of growing hostility toward him.

a. summary statement, 1:14-15

This is a very important passage. The decisive moment for God's action has come. *The whole New Testament can be seen as an expansion of these two verses.*

Mark sets the beginning of Jesus' ministry at the time of John's arrest. The word for "time" here means the right time, the decisive moment. In Galatians 4:4, Paul has a similar idea. To say the time is fulfilled is to say that the ministry of Jesus Christ is part of a divine plan, part of God's whole purpose for the redemption of the world.

"Kingdom of God" does not mean an earthly utopia or a just social order; it is God's sovereignty or rule, breaking in now, and shortly to be fully revealed. It is at hand, very near. It is a gift of a new kind of personal and corporate life that God is giving to man. In some of the parables, the emphasis falls on its being already present: see 4:3-9, 26-29, 30-32. But this is not Mark's main emphasis, as it is, for example, in the Fourth Gospel. Mark's position is that the kingdom is here, yet not quite here, and he maintains this tension throughout. God is in the process of doing a decisive thing for men. Jesus asks: Do you wish to understand and receive it? Two things are necessary: repent and believe in the Gospel. To repent is not merely to be sorry for mistakes, it is to make a radical break with one's present way of life. "Believe" means to give oneself in complete trust and obedience to God who is making himself known in the work of Jesus Christ.

b. the first disciples are called, 1:16-20

The kingdom of God has been announced, and now there is work to be done on its behalf. The Christian faith is not only an individual affair, it also involves a new kind of community. Two groups of two each are summoned first. Notice the "immediately" of verses 18 and 20. Mark likes to use this word, and it gives a note of urgency to his narrative. Perhaps the first readers of the gospel were expected to learn from the immediacy of the response here: no time for excuses. Christ calls, and men follow at once.

It is probable that from verse 16 to the end of this chapter we have a continuous narrative of a single 24-hour period in the early ministry of Jesus.

c. at Capernaum, 1:21-39

1. the demoniac in the synagogue, 1:21-28

The thing that astonishes the hearers is Jesus' direct claim to be speaking for God and his refusal to cite traditional authorities for his teaching, as the scribes did.

A mentally deranged man approaches him, apparently with some fear. Without any elaborate gestures, Jesus cures the man. Again people are astonished, not that he could quiet a demoniac—many exorcists at this time did that—but that he did it so simply with only a word of command. The convulsions of verse 26 suggest epilepsy. Apparently there is a power in Jesus that some can already discern, and, oddly enough, the poor madman is able to perceive it, though the disciples never fully understood it until after the resurrection.

This is the first of many stories of healing in this gospel. We have to remember that physical evil or disease in biblical times had two possible interpretations. One, that it was a punishment for sin (Job's friends take this position in their argument, and see also John 9:2); another, that the demons visited even good men and took control of them. We must try to understand the meaning of these narratives before we too easily reject them. The healings must be seen as signs of the emerging rule or kingdom of God (see Matthew 12:28), and also as expressions of Jesus' concern for the physical (as well as the spiritual) part of a man. Before we become too certain that things like this cannot happen, we might want to look at more recent claims for spiritual healing. And we ought to add that we make nonsense of the gospel story if we arbitrarily drop out all the healing "miracles." Each one must be studied on its own merits.

2. *Peter's mother-in-law, 1:29-31*

This incident takes place at Peter's home in

Capernaum, and the lifelike detail suggests that it comes from the recollection of·Peter himself. Notice the woman's response of gratitude after her fever is relieved.

3. *other healings that evening,* 1:32-34

The sun has set, and the Sabbath is technically over, so now devout Jews may bring their sick to Jesus without fear of breaking the law. Again the demons seem to have a special insight into the character of Jesus, and he forbids them to speak.

4. *withdrawal and return,* 1:35-39

After a day of healing and preaching, Jesus withdraws for prayer. We must be careful in our interpretation of Christ that we do not make improbable or unreal his habit of prayer to the Father. He prayed because he needed to pray.

d. *the cure of a leper,* 1:40-45

This may not have been a case of what we

call leprosy; more likely it was a skin disease like eczema. The phrase "moved with pity" in verse 41 probably read "moved with anger" in the original, and has here been toned down by Mark. What was it that angered Jesus? Not the interruption surely; not even the man's implied doubt of Jesus' willingness to cure him. Perhaps this anger describes Jesus' reaction to the disease itself. Jesus bids the man follow the Jewish laws controlling leprosy: to go directly to the priest so that the cure can be verified, and to be silent about the cure in public. But the man disobeyed, and Jesus is again restricted in his movements.

e. conflicts with the scribes, 2:1—3:6

1. the paralytic and forgiveness, 2:1-12

There is a break of a few days. Jesus returns to Capernaum, where he had been staying, perhaps at Peter's house. Four men bearing another man on a stretcher approach. Unable to make their way through the crowd at the front door, they go up to the roof by an outside stairway. Making an opening in the roof (made of branches and mud), they lower the man into Jesus' presence. Jesus comments on their faith, and pronounces the paralytic's sins forgiven.

We must remember that one of the traditional explanations of disease is that it is caused by sin. In forgiving the sick man, he assumes that man's physical and spiritual needs are all of a piece.

The claim to forgive is what offends the scribes. Only God can forgive, so these words of Jesus are blasphemy to them. Jesus discerns their objections, and in addition to forgiving the man, cures him as well. Now the Messiah was not expected to forgive sins in Jewish thought, so the scribes are not faced with a messianic claim. This is something more serious: a claim to a direct and unique relation to God himself. Two miracles have taken place: a man has been healed, and a man has received the divine pardon through Jesus. Both healing and forgiveness are God's work, so Jesus is acting out indirectly, rather than explicitly declaring, his meaning and status.

"Son of man" in verse 10 is the first occurrence of this important phrase. It comes from Daniel 7:13, where the seer sees a human figure receiving power and glory at God's hands. The title originally, therefore, suggests a supernatural divine figure, and it was not commonly used for the Messiah. Jesus takes this picture of the heavenly man, and fuses with it the conception of the humble and suffering servant from Isaiah 53. The Son of man comes to earth and suffers and dies at the hands of lawless men. This double conception is the clue to the mystery of Jesus' messiahship. Sometimes Mark's use of "Son of man" points to the exalted and heavenly figure (8:38, 14:62), sometimes the humility is emphasized (8:31, 10:45).

2. the call of Levi, 2:13-14

The methods of tax collecting in those days
gave a good deal of opportunity for graft,
and tax collectors as a group were generally
disliked. A Jew in this position would have
broken the law forbidding physical contact
with the Gentile. Levi here has traditionally
been identified with Matthew, the author of
the first gospel, but one cannot be certain
of this.

3. eating with tax collectors and sinners, 2:15-17

"Sinners" refers to all those who fell short of
the rigorous Pharisaic interpretation of the
law. Some of the scribes belonging to the
strict Pharisee party accused the disciples:
Why does he eat with such riffraff? Jesus'
reply has a note of irony. A physician can do
nothing for the sick if he doesn't seek them
out to help them. You, he remarks to the
Pharisees, are of course righteous men and

need no healing. But the Gospel of the kingdom is for sinners, not for those who think
they are righteous. There is a hint here, as
in the whole of Jesus' profound analysis of
self-righteousness, that the man who thinks
he is righteous is worse off than the man who
admits his need.

Jesus' response in verse 17 has an exact
parallel in Paul's great summary of the Gospel in Romans 5:8: "God shows his love for
us in that while we were yet sinners Christ
died for us."

4. fasting, 2:18-22

John's disciples were a distinct group for
some time after their master's arrest and
death, and they and the Pharisees both made
a practice of fasting, though it was not required by Jewish law. Jesus is asked why his
disciples do not do the same. Verse 20
clearly refers to Jesus' death, though no one
understands it as such. There is no reason to
suspect that this veiled reference to Jesus'

death was added later. Jesus already has confronted his opponents in controversy, and soon (in 3:6) we read that a plan to destroy him is being discussed.

5. *on the Sabbath,* 2:23-28

Here the disciples are accused by the Pharisees of breaking the law prohibiting the reaping of grain on the Sabbath. Jesus responds with an argument based on their own authority, the scriptures. If David could take food on the Sabbath for his hungry men, surely the disciples are entitled to do the same. Human need takes precedence over the law. The final phrase, ". . . the Son of man is lord even of the Sabbath," does not mean that any man is master over the law. It means that Jesus Christ as the Son of man, God's unique messenger, is lord of the Sabbath and its laws. Why? Because with him the messianic age has dawned, and the Sabbath laws may be put aside during this time of joy. This does not mean that disciples, then or now, do not need law for the regulation of their moral lives. Because of our weakness, we shall always need the correction of the law. It does mean, however, that in Jesus Christ we see not a new set of laws but a new kind of divine love. Christ's love is always destructive of even the best human law and goodness; this is why he was so dangerous then, and it is why Christianity is always potentially a revolutionary threat.

6. the man with the withered hand, 3:1-6

Here Jesus himself, and not the disciples as above, is accused of breaking a law which required that only in extreme emergency could acts of healing be performed on the Sabbath. He answers with a direct and unanswerable counterquestion.

After these two clear instances of violation of their traditions, the Pharisees have apparently made up their minds about Jesus (see verse 6). The Herodians mentioned here

were a conservative Jewish group that hoped
for a restoration of the monarchy of Herod.
Here is the first clear warning of tragedy to
come; the shadow of the cross is already
hanging over these early events.

2. the second phase of the ministry in Galilee, 3:7—6:13

a. summary statement: the crowds by the lake, 3:7-12

In spite of the growing hostility that has
forced Jesus to carry on his work outside
the towns by the lakeside, a large crowd
continues to listen to him.

b. appointment of the twelve, 3:13-19

These verses mark a decisive moment in the
ministry and in the history of the Christian
church. In this section, we begin with the
appointment of the twelve disciples, and
close with their mission. The number 12 may
well be significant: there were twelve tribes

in Israel, and the disciples are to be the beginning of a new Israel, the new people of God, the church. In verse 14, we find the twofold task of the disciple. For a while at the beginning he was to stay with Jesus, to learn, listen, and understand. But later he was to be sent out to do the same work Jesus was already doing—preaching the Gospel of the kingdom, and healing the broken bodies and minds of men. This has always been the double task of the Christian community, not merely the task of its official leaders. (A fundamental difference between the Protestant and the Roman Catholic can be discerned here: to the question, "Who is the legitimate successor to the disciple?" the Protestant answers: the body of believers, the church. The Roman Catholic answers in terms of the priestly hierarchy.)

Peter is a name that means "the rock." This may refer to his rugged character and appearance, or it may refer to his position as a foundation of the church, an early witness to the resurrection. "Sons of thunder" may have something to do with the volatile tempers of James and John. The meaning of "Cananaean" is probably "Zealot"—a member of an extreme nationalist group of Pharisees which hoped to drive the Romans from the country by force.

c. charges against Jesus, 3:19-35

Back home, eating with his family and friends, Jesus is still claimed by the crowds. He gives himself so intensely to the needs of the crowd that his family suspects he is out of his mind. "Friends" in verse 21 probably should read "family." Apparently the local Pharisees have called some scribes down from Jerusalem to observe Jesus, and they enter the controversy. Playing on the suspicions of the family, they suggest that Jesus is possessed by the prince of demons, Satan himself. They cannot deny his power to heal, but they suggest that this power is a devilish one, not divine. (Of course, if

Jesus is not what he claims to be, the scribes are right. He *is* mad, dangerously deluded, and he has deceived well-meaning people ever since.)

Jesus replies with two brief parables. Satan is in charge of a kingdom of evil. Why should he stir up division within this kingdom, if I am part of it, Jesus asks. Since I am engaged in a battle against the kingdom of evil, I can hardly be on the side of the head of that kingdom. The strong man's house and goods, in the second parable, refer to Satan and his possession of men. Jesus himself is the one who enters and binds the strong man by casting out demons and freeing men from evil and disease.

The passage in verses 28-30 on the unforgivable sin has often caused sensitive people much distress. Jesus makes it clear what that sin is: ascribing to the devil what belongs to God, making evil into a god. Jesus may not be directly accusing his family and the scribes of committing such a sin, but he does suggest that they are close to it. The apparent harshness of this saying must be set alongside verse 28 with its emphasis that all sins, even blasphemy, will be forgiven.

This section concludes in verses 31-35 with a saying about the true family of Jesus. It is hard not to discern here a note of disappointment in Jesus' attitude toward his mother and brothers. Tradition has sometimes tried to explain away this direct reference to Jesus' brothers; some have tried to say that they were half brothers or cousins. But there is no possible escape from the meaning of the word; they are his true brothers, the younger sons of Mary. It is probable that Mark knows nothing of the virgin birth tradition; this story of course neither supports nor denies it.

Whoever is obedient to God's will is the true family of Jesus. If the actual family do not understand him, they are no longer his true family. This must have come home with real comfort to the persecuted church in

Mark's day, with its broken families and temptations to recant based on family loyalty.

d. what is a parable, and why is it used?, 4:1-34

This chapter contains several parables, an interpretation of a parable, and some remarks on their significance and use. Several things should be noted on the parable form itself. Jesus did not invent it (it is found in the Old Testament; see II Samuel 12:1-6), but he gave it its highest expression. In essence a parable is a comparison, usually of God or the kingdom of God to some ordinary event or thing. It must be distinguished from allegory in which every detail of the story has symbolic significance. The parable has but one point to make, and the descriptive details are not independently important except as they clarify the single point and the response that is expected.

1. the sower, 4:1-9

This parable can be seen as Jesus' reflection on the progress of his mission in Galilee, its success and failure. The seed is the Gospel of the kingdom; but it is responded to in different ways. Its reception depends on the kind of soil that receives it. In verse 9, a sense of responsibility is impressed on the hearers, as if to say: make sure that your response is like the last one, the good soil bringing forth fruit.

2. the purpose of parables, 4:10-12

Later, when they are alone with Jesus, the disciples ask about the purpose of Jesus' parabolic teaching. Jesus replies that parables are meant to conceal the truth from the unprepared so that they might receive the judgment they deserve, and not repent and be forgiven.

Some observers defend the saying, calling it hard but true. They point to Isaiah 6:9-10 (which is reflected in verse 12 here), where the prophet looks back on his unsuccessful career and sees his failure as God's will.

Others admit that Mark wrote what stands, but they find the idea intolerable and wrong. Jesus, they say, clearly uses the parables to convey and elucidate truth, not to conceal it. He is not interested in transmitting secret information to a select few: he seeks to bring all people to a knowledge of the Gospel. So though we can understand why Mark could come to this curious view (perhaps at the close of a career as an apostle that did not have the success he had expected), we must reject it as a true reflection of Jesus' mind, and as out of keeping with the other things we know about his teaching.

The reader today must come to his own decision on this matter, and it will have to be based very largely on his over-all picture of Christ in the gospels.

A word should be added here about the

idea of the "secret" that appears in verse 11. It is a favorite idea of Mark's, and it is responsible for both the dramatic intensity and the theological depth of his gospel. He means by this idea that the true character of Christ as Son of God and bearer of the kingdom, as suffering and dying Messiah, is not obvious to everyone. Indeed, it is scarcely obvious even to the disciples. Peter partly sees it and largely misses it in 8:29-33. And supremely, the Jewish leaders are blind to the true meaning of Christ. This is not because of mere ignorance; Mark sees it as God's deliberate withholding of true understanding. The secret must not be revealed until the proper time, until men are prepared to receive it.

Here is the best explanation for the otherwise rather puzzling advice that Jesus constantly gives to those he has cured, not to speak publicly of what has been done to them. Sometimes, it may be, this advice can be interpreted as a word of caution to avoid bringing the inevitable crisis to pass prematurely. But the best way of viewing this advice is to see it as part of Mark's over-all theological structure. Jesus knew himself to be the Messiah, and he acts out his true nature in incident after incident. But the whole picture needed the completion of the death and the resurrection. Hence the idea of the secret, part of Jesus' own teaching, is rightly underlined by Mark as he presents his full portrait of his master.

3. an interpretation of the parable, 4:13-20

Two factors have led many observers to label this an early church homily on "how to hear God's word," rather than a direct transcription of Jesus' own words. (1) It is allegorized, which Jesus rarely does with his parables; (2) from verse 17 on, there are clear references to the situation of the church in Mark's day under the persecution of the emperor Nero. The references to persecution and tribulation, the remarks about worldly cares

and security choking out the original fervor,
probably reflect the difficulties facing the
church at the time of the writing of the gospel rather than thirty years before. But there
is no reason to believe that some interpretation of the basic parable was not given by
Jesus. Mark is here shaping his material so
that it would speak as directly as possible
to his fellow Christians under the sentence
of death.

4. other parables and sayings, 4:21-34

The section in verses 21-25 is another ex-
hortation to respond to the preaching of the
kingdom. Even if the kingdom is partly hid-
den now, it will shortly be revealed to all.

In the little parable of verses 26-29, the
kingdom of God is again compared to a seed.
Here the point is that just as the growth of a
seed is not a process man controls, so the
kingdom of God is not a human achievement
but a gift of God. But note: when the grain
is ripe, man must harvest it. The kingdom

of God is now ripe; it is fully present, and man is not to sit back and wait, he is to choose it. The critical time is at hand. This parable, then, is more than a description of the kingdom of God; it is a call for immediate decision.

The parable of the mustard seed in verses 30-32 has two points: (1) just as the tiny mustard seed can grow (in the Mediterranean area) into a fairly tall tree, so the humble start of the kingdom of God does not preclude a victorious ending; (2) the kingdom is now present, and all nations and peoples ("birds of the air" was a phrase used by the rabbis to mean all people, including Gentiles) may now partake of it. Verses 33-34 serve as a conclusion to this whole section on parables and their meaning.

e. a group of miracle stories, 4:35—5:43

1. the storm on the lake, 4:35-41

The disciples and Jesus now cross the Sea of Galilee, from the west to the east shore. The

detailed description here suggests an eyewit-
ness account. A number of boats set sail; in
one of them, Jesus goes to sleep on the steers-
man's cushion in the stern. A lake storm
blows up, and the disciples rouse Jesus with
a slightly bitter question. He speaks a word
to the winds and the waves, and the storm
subsides. He then rebukes the others for
their fear, which he defines as lack of trust in
God's care. They in turn respond with another kind of fear, a sort of awe in the presence of the one they only dimly understand
as their Lord. The disciples' question in verse
41 presupposes, in Mark's mind, the answer:
This is the Son of God at work. The contrast
between faithless fear and genuine fear of
the Lord is instructive. This story must certainly have served as a message of hope to
the storm-tossed church under persecution in
Mark's day.

But this story is also what we call a nature
miracle, and it is difficult for us today, even
after we have understood its original mean-

ing and use. The healing miracles are hard enough, but there are some things in our experience that help us start on an understanding of them. The details of this story, on the other hand, seem incredible to modern man. What are we to say about it?

Some have tried to rationalize it. What Jesus really calmed, it is said, is the storm of fear in the disciples' hearts. Or, the whole thing was coincidence, even though the disciples wrongly assumed a cause and effect relation. This sort of explaining away gets rid of modern difficulties well enough, but it will hardly do, for the good reason that it departs from the simple sense of the text, which interprets the stilling of the storm as a miracle of divine providence, and as such we must deal with it.

To be sure, the ancient world was not inclined to think of the universe as bound by what we call "natural law," and so it did not have the problem with miracles that a scientific age has. What are stumbling blocks for us were merely evidences of God's action for them. But this story is really about God's power and his care for men, and not mainly about a miraculous calm. And surely we do not believe any less in the power and love of God for men than did biblical man.

Don't we pray for natural events to come to pass? For the safety of travelers, for rain, for healing of loved ones? Do we believe that God raised Jesus Christ from the dead? If we really believe that in Christ God was truly active and present, does this story present insuperable difficulties? In any case, we must be careful that we allow our Christian presuppositions to have as much weight in our reading of such narratives as we allow our modern scientific ones. Our real understanding of this story, and of others like it in Mark, will emerge not as we ask the question: "Can natural laws be broken?", but only as we reflect on a far more fundamental question: "What do we mean by Jesus Christ as Son of God?"

2. *the Gerasene madman, 5:1-20*

Here is another story of an exorcism, but one with more details than usual, and more difficulties. We are in Gentile territory; it is unlikely that a herd of pigs would be found on Jewish land. On the east shore of the lake Jesus meets a maniac who had been ostracized from his village and forced to live in the cemetery on the outskirts of town. The man sees Jesus, runs to him, and in fear and awe falls at his feet. Again the demons (that is, the demon-possessed man) recognize the divine status of Christ. The man seems to discern in Jesus' wholeness a threat to his brokenness, and implores him to leave him alone. My name is Legion, he remarks bitterly, which means that he has not one but many demons in him.

It seems that the man tries to compromise with Jesus: don't send any evil spirits out of the country, send them into the pigs. (Observe the confusion of pronouns here; "he" and "they" are mixed up together; the man is both one with his demons and apart from them.) Jesus does so, and the pigs tumble down a cliff into the sea.

The report of this spreads at once, and the townspeople come to observe the cured man. They are now, it seems, afraid of Jesus rather than the ex-maniac; if such a man could destroy swine, what else might he do? He is asked to leave. The man himself asks to come with Jesus, but instead he is told to return home (to a Gentile town, remember, which explains why there would be no danger in proclaiming the cure) and tell people what *God* has done for him. Instead, he tells people what *Jesus* did. (The Decapolis, in verse 20, was a league of ten Greek cities stretching from Damascus to the Arabian desert.)

One problem in this is the sending of the demons into the pigs. Did Jesus deliberately will this? A humanitarian might object that such an act was unnecessarily cruel to pigs.

But to the Jew and to the early Christians who had been Jews the pig was unclean. And if the demons had not been sent into the pigs, it was believed, they would have entered into some other person.

Although the vivid details of this story give it a ring of plausibility, there may be elements of folk legend in it that attached to it before it came into Mark's hands. But behind the difficult details of this story, a basic truth stands. Jesus Christ, then and now, bears a unique divine power that is able to heal all kinds of human brokenness and distortion. We, like the demoniac, may be afraid to be made whole; but when this fear is overcome, wholeness, health, salvation are readily available.

3. *the daughter of Jairus, and the woman with the flow of blood, 5:21-43*

a. Jairus' daughter: introduction, 5:21-24

Jesus crosses back to the western shore,

and a distinguished leader of the synagogue approaches him for help. The man's trust appealed to Jesus, and he goes off with him.

b. the woman with the flow of blood, 5:24-34

On the road to Jairus' house, a great crowd collects and follows Jesus. Among them is a woman with a chronic hemorrhage who had heard of Jesus and who decided to push her way through the crowd to touch him. (Notice how Luke the doctor, in 8:43, tones down Mark's disparaging reference to the medical profession when he writes up the same story.) She approaches him fearfully because she was unclean according to law, and her touch had made Jesus unclean as well. Note that it is the woman's faith—her boldness and trust—that Jesus describes as the means of the cure.

We cannot wholly explain this story;

the vivid details give it an authentic flavor. Autosuggestion is hardly an explanation that will satisfy. Mark's explanation may well be the most plausible one: she was healed because of her confidence in the power of the Son of God.

c. Jairus' daughter: conclusion, 5:35-43

The simple conclusion to the story of Jairus' daughter serves as Mark's climax to the whole group of miracle stories that began with the stilling of the storm.

The report comes, while they are on the way to the house, that the girl has died. Verse 35 suggests that Jesus was not expected to be able to raise the dead. Silencing the professional mourners outside the house, Jesus takes the inner group of favorite disciples with him to the girl's side. She rises from the bed at his word, and he reminds them to feed her.

The question raised by verse 39 is this:

Was the girl truly dead, or merely in a coma? Did Jesus believe she was really dead? Did Mark? Jesus had not seen the child, so it is hard to believe he was making a diagnosis in verse 39. Mark apparently believes, in placing this incident as a climax to the whole group of miracle stories, that this was an instance of a raising from the dead. The greatest reserve must be exercised before we explain away or rationalize what is difficult for us. The most important question, again, that this story poses is this: What is the meaning of Jesus Christ that shines through this incident?

f. a cool reception at home, 6:1-6

Jesus now leaves Capernaum to begin preaching in the villages and towns of Galilee. "His own country" in verse 1 probably means his birthplace, suggesting that Mark did not know of the tradition locating Jesus' birth in Bethlehem. The presence of the disciples suggests that the visit was not for personal reasons.

Many observers believe that verse 3 as it reads has been altered to fit in with the virgin birth tradition, and there is some evidence that the earlier version may have read: "Is not this the son of the carpenter (Joseph) and Mary?"

Because of the cool reception, it is said that Jesus could perform no healings in Nazareth. Not a physical inability, but a spiritual refusal, since the requisite faith and trust was not present. The clause beginning "except . . ." in verse 5 looks like a later editorial addition inserted to soften the suggestion of weakness on Jesus' part.

g. *the sending out of the twelve, 6:6-13*

This is the mission for which the disciples have been called and trained. They are sent out in pairs to heal and to preach the Gospel (verse 12). They are to travel light and to observe certain rules of hospitality. If they are not accepted, they are to leave at once. The shaking off of the dust is a symbolic gesture indicating a rejection of those who reject the message.

III. The Ministry Outside Galilee
6:14—8:26

1. Herod's fears, and the murder of John the Baptist, 6:14-29

Mark uses this section as an interlude to fill up the time during which the disciples are out on their mission. Of course, the death of John the Baptist probably was deeply significant to Jesus, and may have underscored his own forebodings about the future.

Herod hears of the mission of Jesus, and asks about him. (He is not technically a king, but tetrarch of Galilee and Perea, ruler of one-quarter of the realm of his father, the late King Herod the Great.) With a murderer's superstition, he fears Jesus as John the Baptist come to life again. After an introduction, Mark recounts what is doubtless a popular legend about John's death. The historian Josephus, writing some sixty years after the event, gives a number of different details. Here John has been imprisoned because of his opposition to Herod's adulterous marriage to his brother's wife Herodias. (We do not know if the brother was alive or dead; or, if alive, divorced from Herodias or not.) Herodias wanted to kill John, but the prophet apparently exercised a sort of fascination for Herod, and he merely imprisoned him. But Herodias seizes a chance at a party to trick Herod (probably in his cups) into decreeing John's death. Salome is the name given to the daughter by Josephus, but there is no name here. The note of remorse in verse 26 is interesting, but he keeps his promise and orders the execution.

2. *the feeding of the 5,000 and its sequels, 6:30—7:37*

a. the feeding of the 5,000, 6:30-44

The twelve now return from their mission, and Jesus takes them away to a quiet place for a rest. But the crowds follow along, and Jesus speaks with them until it is time for the evening meal. The disciples ironically ask Jesus if they should go into the village and buy forty dollars' worth of bread for the crowd. He takes the food he and the disciples have brought along for their meal, blesses it, and distributes it to the crowd. They are all filled, and there are twelve (symbolic number?) baskets of food left over.

The story, as Mark received it, was clearly a miracle, in spite of the absence of any note of astonishment or wonder in the narrative. But it is more than a creative miracle of God as it stands. It is also a sign, a pointer to a deeper truth (see Mark 6:52). When John writes up this incident in the fourth gospel (Chapter 6) he follows it with a discourse about the bread of life. The kingdom of God is, in other places, likened to a feast: Luke 14:16-24 and Matthew 22:1-14. And there are hints here that remind us of the last supper, so that this can be read as a kind of preview of that (compare 6:41 and 14:22).

So we cannot know whether the original event was miraculous or not. There is a note of mystery here, and it is best not to be sure of any conclusion. However, almost anything is better than the explanation one sometimes hears: that this is a lesson in sharing—Jesus began to share his food, and everyone else decided to do the same!

b. crossing the lake, 6:45-52

Jesus asks the disciples to leave the site of the feeding and after he has dispersed the crowd he retires into the hills for prayer. A storm blows up, and the disciples in the boats see Jesus apparently walking on the water. He quiets their fear and enters a boat, but the disciples still do not understand.

We have some grounds for attempting to rationalize this story, for there is no particular meaning to the story if read as a miracle.

The disciples were in trouble, and what fright-
ened them even more than the storm was the
ghostly figure of Jesus himself. The picture of
Jesus in the story is somewhat unreal. It may
be that the disciples were some time in get-
ting under way against the wind, that Jesus
unexpectedly waded out into the shallow
surf to meet them, and that he took them by
surprise. The word of comfort in verse 50
is the significant part, and Mark adds his
favorite idea about the disciples' slowness
and immaturity.

c. landing on the other side, 6:53-56

Notice the growing popularity described here.

d. more controversy with the Pharisees, 7:1-23

This whole section concerns the nature of
religious defilement, and verse 15 is the
key to the whole. The passage can be con-
veniently broken up into three sections.

1. on the washing of hands, 7:1-8

The Pharisees, along with some visiting observers from Jerusalem, question Jesus' rejection of the fairly recent Jewish practice of ceremonial washing before meals. As is so often the case, Jesus does not directly respond to the question, but goes straight to the real issue at stake, which he rightly sees to be the authority of scribal tradition. (Mark remembers he is writing for Gentiles unfamiliar with Jewish practice, so he adds verses 3 and 4.) The quotation from scripture in verses 6 and 7 gives Jesus' position.

2. "Corban," 7:9-13

Again he gives an example of how human traditions can take false precedence over the commandment of God. The fifth commandment of Moses is this: Honor your father and mother. But you scribes, he says, fully approve when an unscrupulous son makes a vow to dedicate all his income to the temple, depriving his poor parents of their only means of support. "Corban" means "dedicated to God." So, a perfectly valid human vow of dedication can be used in an irresponsible way which breaks a far more basic commandment of God.

3. more sayings on defilement, 7:14-23

Verse 15 is the summary here, and it is a very significant passage for personal ethics. This is a decisive blow against all legalism: things or places cannot be unclean, only persons. Persons are not defiled by other things, but by themselves and their own disobedience to God. There is no inherent evil in nature, the world, or material things in the Christian ethic. Sin lies in man, and in his misuse of himself and the good things of God's creation. Compare this passage with Jesus' more detailed analysis of man's relation to material possessions in Matthew 6:19-34. Verses 18-19 are a rather unimaginative interpretation of the first half of verse

15, perhaps reflecting the ethical teaching of the early church. Verses 20-23 are a somewhat better interpretation of the second half of verse 15.

e. two healings, 7:24-37

1. meeting a Greek woman, 7:24-30

Again Jesus' search for privacy is interrupted. The harshness of the reply in verse 27 to the woman's request for help is the main difficulty here. Some find here a reflection of the early Christian (that is, Jewish-Christian) prejudice against Gentiles. Some find a genuine tension in Jesus' own mind between the claims of the Jews and Gentiles. Some find in Jesus' words merely a half-playful testing of the woman's faith. Jesus is impressed, in any case, by her clever and bold reply, and the cure is effected. This is a fairly rare instance of a cure done at a distance. But the real issue here is not healing so much as it is the relation of the Jew and the Gentile in the kingdom of God.

2. *the deaf man with a speech defect,* *7:31-37*

The unusual gestures and the use of spittle (a traditional habit of ancient exorcists) can perhaps be explained by the man's deafness: he is unable to hear the usual word of command and healing.

The sighing in verse 34 is a trace of Jesus' profound compassion for the sufferer, and perhaps also of anger at the infirmity itself. Mark doubtless has in mind the passage describing the messianic age in Isaiah 35:5-10. So the evangelist here invites us to look beyond the relief of human suffering to a mighty act of God's chosen servant, bringing the kingdom into history and dethroning the rule of evil in the world.

3. *the feeding of the 4,000 and its sequels,* *8:1-26*

a. *the feeding of the 4,000, 8:1-10*

Many scholars believe that this feeding is

not a second incident of a miraculous feeding, but a variant account of the same event. Perhaps Mark intended the first feeding to symbolize the salvation of the Jews, and this one that of the Gentiles, since it takes place on Gentile soil. It is difficult to explain the disciples' question in 8:4 if there had been a recent incident similar to this.

The parallelism between the contexts of both feeding stories is interesting to note:

6:34-44,	feeding the 5,000	8:1-9,	feeding of 4,000
6:53-56,	crossing the Gennesaret	8:10,	crossing the sea to Dalmanutha
7:1-23,	controversy with Pharisees and scribes on defilement	8:11-13,	controversy with Pharisees about signs
7:24-30,	the Greek woman (throwing bread to the dogs)	8:14-21,	sayings about bread
7:31-37,	healing a deaf stammerer	8:22-26,	healing a blind man

There are also a number of differences between the accounts. Here we have seven loaves instead of five, 4,000 instead of 5,000, compassion because of the people's hunger here, compassion because they are like sheep without a shepherd in the earlier narrative

b. the Pharisees ask about a sign, 8:11-13

Paul said (I Corinthians 1:22) that the Greeks seek after wisdom and the Jews look for signs. Here the Pharisees want some visible proofs of Jesus' claims; a tangible, and possibly supernatural, portent. Jesus refuses to give this sort of proof, though Mark clearly believes that as the supernatural Son of God he could have done so had he wished.

c. the mystery of the loaves, 8:14-21

In reading this section, regard verse 15 as a footnote: a warning to beware of the evil influence of the Pharisees and of Herod. It is probably an independent saying that was dropped in here because of the relationship of the ideas of leaven and bread.

The disciples have forgotten to bring along food for their boat trip across the sea. Jesus uses this incident to censure them for their forgetfulness about the meaning of the bread in the miraculous feeding. Here we have an interpretation that approaches the kind of thing the author of the fourth gospel does regularly. Mark shows us here how these feeding stories were understood by the early Christians. The feeding was a sign that the kingdom of God was in their midst and that God was sufficient for their needs. This story reminded the early church readers that not even the disciples understood what was happening in their midst. Perhaps, Mark is saying, some of us today do not yet understand the mystery of the loaves.

d. a blind man is healed, 8:22-26

Here is a cure much like that of the deaf stammerer; it is done in private, and spittle is used. It seemed to be a difficult cure to effect, for it required a second laying on of hands.

There is real artistry in Mark's placing this

story here, following the one before. He has just told us of the disciples' blindness to the meaning of the loaves. Now he tells us here that even the blind can be made to see. The blind man saw; the disciples would come to see clearly; and Mark's readers will come to see as well.

IV. What Peter Finally Learned; the Journey to Jerusalem

8:27—10:52

1. *messiahship and suffering, 8:27—9:29*

a. *Peter's confession; the Messiah must suffer, 8:27-33*

Here is a crucial turning-point in the gospel. Jesus had not yet openly declared himself to be the Messiah, he had rather tried to "act it out" to his disciples. Now he seems to think they are prepared to go more deeply. Peter, who up to now had shown no special insight (and who likewise did not show much insight later), blurts out what many of them must have been thinking. As when the demons had recognized him, Jesus bids them all be silent about this new insight.

As soon as they have come to recognize his messiahship, Jesus takes them a step further with verse 31. For traditional Judaism "Messiah" meant the future king of Israel, powerful and victorious over all foes. Here Jesus declares that his kind of Messiah means suffering and death. The "must" in verse 31 is a divine necessity, and it comes not only from Jesus' acute estimate of the forces already set against him but also from his meditation on the great suffering servant passage of Isaiah 53 which he was beginning to see as a clue to his own ministry and life.

The idea of a Messiah who must suffer gets Peter out of his depth. He protests, and Jesus rebukes him.

Verse 31 represents the first of three predictions of the death and resurrection (the others are in 9:31 and 10:33-34). Mark places these sayings in their contexts to show that Jesus foresaw his sufferings and death, and this is certainly true. But to many it seems difficult to believe that Jesus predicted his own resurrection. The disciples do not seem to grasp these words; and at the crucifixion they flee in despair as if they had never heard them.

So here, something of the mystery of the Gospel is being dispelled. Jesus is the Christ, but in a different sense than anyone expected. A public announcement of the messiahship, therefore, without this deeper interpretation of it, would be foolhardy. The point of this section, then, is not merely that Peter confesses Jesus as the Christ; but also that to be the Christ, the Messiah, means to suffer and die.

b. the meaning of discipleship, 8:34—9:1

Here is a collection of sayings on the meaning of following Jesus. Notice their location immediately after the revelation of the inevitable suffering of the Messiah. Remember, too, the suffering that the persecuted Christians of Mark's day were having to undergo.

There are three conditions of true discipleship: self-denial is the first one (verse 34), which does not mean giving up *things*—as we try to do during Lent—but rather the giving up of our claim to control our lives and handing them to God. It is a confession that our wills for our lives need not be done, and that God's will shall be done, even if it denies what we wish. The second condition is taking up the cross. Bearing the cross has become trivialized in our day; it can often mean simply being brave when things go wrong. But in Jesus' words here, to be a disciple is to be willing to live and show forth the kind of suffering love that shines through the cross. To take up the cross is to acknowledge that discipleship may not win the plaudits of the world and bring to man the gifts of gratitude and success that the world can offer. Following Jesus is the last condition. This is not a lifeless imitation, but a decision to identify ourselves as radically as he did with both God's will and the suffering and need of men. This is a following that may lead to death. Verse 35 is the great paradox of biblical religion. "Saves" here means "seeks anxiously to preserve." Losing life does not mean merely death, but giving one's life up completely into God's hands. Verse 38 speaks of the consequences of disloyalty to Christ. The reference is to the last judgment. Does Jesus refer to the supernatural Son of man as another than himself or as himself?

c. the transfiguration, and coming down from the mountain, 9:2-13

This difficult story is sometimes interpreted as an historical incident in which the true glory of Christ was revealed to the three disciples, sometimes as a vision, and sometimes as a legend with only symbolic meaning.

It will help if we look at this as the counterpart for the disciples of Jesus' experience at baptism. Whatever happened, whatever a camera would or would not have recorded (and both a total acceptance as historical and a confident rejection as legendary are unwise), a significant moment in the disciples' understanding of Christ is portrayed. The relation of Christ to the Old Testament law and prophets is part of this new insight. Peter at first wants them all on the same level, and Mark (verse 6) apologizes for Peter's foolishness.

In verses 9-13 the disciples ask Jesus some further questions about what has happened. (Put the second half of verse 12 after verse 10; this will clear up the order a little.) They are wondering about rising from the dead, the suffering Messiah, and the relation of the Messiah to John the Baptist. The scribes have apparently been discussing the idea of the Messiah with the disciples, and their case against Jesus' claims apparently involves the fact that since a new Elijah traditionally must come as a forerunner, and since one has not come, Jesus' claims are false. But, Jesus reminds the disciples, the new Elijah has already come in John the Baptist.

d. the epileptic boy, 9:14-29

Jesus and the three disciples who were with him return from the mount of Transfiguration, and the contrast between the divine glory of Christ and the impotence of men (the remaining disciples) could hardly be more striking. The scribes and the disciples are arguing over the latter's failure to cure an epileptic boy. In the conversation with the father, the importance of faith and trust for healing is again emphasized. The honest cry of the father, "I believe, help my unbelief," proves his trust in Jesus, who takes the child by the hand and rouses him from the coma.

Jesus' reply to the disciples' question in verse 28 is instructive. Jesus is depicted in Mark as the Son of God with immediate power over the demons, yet here he says that prayer is essential in healing. This story is an important one for our whole approach to the healing miracles. They are not only wonderful works that proceeded from Jesus as Son of God. Here we see Jesus with such confidence in God that he expects the disciples to be able to heal, and we see him disappointed when they fail.

2. *a journey through Galilee, 9:30-50*

Here we find a rather loosely strung-together group of narratives, all more or less related to the meaning of true discipleship.

In verses 30-32 we notice the second prediction of the death. Why is it that the disciples don't understand? Is it because they are uncertain just to whom Jesus is referring as "Son of man"?

The next passage, verses 33-37, concerns the nature of true greatness. The disciples are embarrassed when Jesus learns that they were arguing about who was the greatest among them. Verse 35 gives his direct reply to this rather unattractive controversy; and the relation of this saying to the idea of the suffering Messiah is obvious. Then, summoning a little child, he makes his meaning even more vivid. True greatness means care for such helpless ones as this child; it means the wonder and humility that the child displays.

(Yet verses 36-37 are not precisely a direct answer to the problem of true greatness. Compare this story with the similar one in 10:13-16. Perhaps 9:36-37 should be the conclusion to the story in Chapter 10, and 10:15 the conclusion to the story here. Mark may have exchanged the two sayings about children.)

The story of the rival healer in 9:38-41 gives a lesson in tolerance. Welcome anyone who acts in my name, Jesus says, even though he is not an official disciple. Is there a conflict between 9:40 and Luke 11:23, or can both be true?

It is difficult to see much order here unless we assume that this is a compilation of Jesus' sayings made by the early church for instructional purposes. Verses 37-41 center around the idea of Jesus' name; 42, 43, 45, 47, and 48 (verses 44 and 46 are left out in the best manuscripts) refer to offenses or causing to sin; 48-50 center around the idea of salt.

3. on the way to Jerusalem, 10:1-52

a. on adultery and divorce, 10:1-12

In the background of this lies an argument between two rival rabbinic schools on divorce. The school of Hillel said that a man could get a divorce for the most trivial of reasons —if a wife burned his food, for example. The stricter school of Shammai declared that only unchastity was a just cause. Both these inter-pretations spring from Deuteronomy 24:1-4. But Jesus cuts beneath all this, and declares that Moses' permission of divorce was a con-cession to human sin and that according to Genesis 1:27 and 2:24, God ordains that the husband and wife shall be indissolubly one. The exceptions to this view, which we find in Matthew 5:32, 19:9, and Luke 16:18, represent the practical needs of the early church modifying Jesus' clear position stated here.

The point of the verses 10-12 is that in Jewish law a woman could be accused of adultery, but a married man could not. Jesus here abolishes the legal exemption of the man. "Against her" in verse 11 means, apparently, against the first wife.

It seems clear that Jesus' own position is accurately reflected in this account, and that it is qualified in Matthew and Luke. But how do we apply this teaching to the complex problem of divorce in the modern world? This is not simple to answer. Some would say that because of this teaching, divorce is simply and unequivocally prohibited. Others would object to this legalistic use of Jesus' words, and would say something like this: What we have from Jesus is the reminder that God's will for marriage is indissoluble union. But sometimes divorce, which is against this divine will, must occur. When it must, there is a sense in which God's will is being violated, even when it seems necessary from the human point of view.

b. on children, 10:13-16

The disciples apparently try to protect Jesus from the children who are being brought to him, and he is sharply indignant. Let them come; we can learn from them how to receive the kingdom of God. It is not the much-talked-about innocence of children (which parents might well question!) that is being commended here, but their sense of dependence and their receptiveness. This is a touching story about children, but even more, it is a parable about the grace of God.

c. on discipleship and riches, 10:17-31

1. the "rich young ruler," 10:17-22

The traditional description of this man is a composite one; "rich" is from Mark 10:22, "young" from Matthew 19:20, and "ruler" from Luke 18:18.

The man kneels before the teacher, a genuine act of reverence, showing that he is in earnest and not trying to trap Jesus with his question. Jesus refuses the word "good," not to say that he is sinful, but that his goodness is not that of God and has to be learned step by step, just as our own does. God alone is truly good, truly sovereign.

After the man says that he has observed all the commandments from his youth, Jesus looks on him with affection, and makes the final demand. But it proves too hard, and the man turns away sadly. This demand must not be taken as a general requirement of discipleship, but as a specific call to a particular man whose money stood in the way of full allegiance.

2. the danger of riches, 10:23-27

Who then can be saved? The answer is simple and fundamental: as an achievement of man, salvation is impossible; as a gift of God, it is available to all. The saying of verse 25 is a humorous exaggeration that underlines the virtual impossibility of a rich man meeting the conditions for receiving God's kingdom.

3. on rewards, 10:28-31

Peter's remark refers to Jesus' final challenge to the young man. Jesus replies that though the disciples have given up their actual families, in the new corporate life of the kingdom a new family will be given, and in the final summing-up of all things, they will enjoy peace and eternal life with God.

d. the third prediction of the Passion, 10:32-34

The details of this prediction correspond closely to the actual events of the passion week, and are probably to be understood as added by Mark for dramatic effect.

The vivid picture of Jesus striding ahead

of his disciples as he makes his way to his fate (verse 32) is an unforgettable scene. Already, the final tragic shape of the drama is beginning to unfold.

e. John and James ask a stupid question, 10:35-45

Just as Peter missed the point of the first prediction of suffering and death, so James and John here completely misunderstand the nature of the kingdom Jesus has been talking about. They conceive of an earthly monarchy, and want to assure themselves of important places. (This is so unflattering a portrait of these two disciples that it cannot be anything but an actual historical reminiscence. The early church would hardly have created this incident.) You will participate in the kingdom, Jesus answers, but only by drinking my cup and being baptized with my baptism. Their ready agreement shows that they miss the identification of "cup" and "baptism" with suffering and death.

Verse 45 is the profound ransom passage, one of the few places in Mark where Jesus interprets the meaning of his own death. Notice how closely the life and the death are related. During the life of Jesus, serving, and not the demand to be served, was the central fact; the death is the final description of the meaning of his life. Behind the idea of ransom is the idea of men in captivity or, as we would say today, kidnapped by sin. Men cannot free themselves, just as a kidnapped victim is not free to release himself, but must wait for the ransom to be paid. The life, and supremely the death, then, serve as God's bearing the sins of men, taking them from men, so that they are no longer bound but free. Here again Jesus sees his own death not only as part of his story, but primarily as the decisive part of a story about God and what He is doing for men.

f. blind Bartimaeus, 10:46-52

The trip to Jerusalem continues. Bartimaeus

gives Jesus a messianic title, Son of David, for now the secret is beginning to leak out. Many try to quiet him, but Jesus does not. In verse 51 Jesus presents the same question to the blind man that he had put just before to James and John (verse 36). It is instructive to compare the two responses. Perhaps Mark wants the reader to see that it is the disciples who are truly blind, and that the blind man has true faith and trust.

V. In Jerusalem Before the Passion
11:1—13:37

1. before the teaching begins, 11:1-25

a. the entry on a donkey, 11:1-11

This entrance into the city is an act of conscious and profound symbolism. Some commentators have compared the entry, the cleansing of the temple, and the last supper to the symbolic gestures of the Old Testament prophets. We are reminded of Jeremiah (Chapter 19) breaking a bottle before his people to symbolize the "breaking" of Jerusalem which he had predicted. The event here has been carefully planned by Jesus, and it may be that the messianic prophecy of Zechariah 9:9 is in his mind. Mark does not refer to this prophecy, though Matthew does in 21:4-5.

It is not so certain that the crowd understands this entry as messianic. The quotation from Psalm 118:26 in verse 9 was employed as a greeting for any pilgrim coming to a religious festival; verse 10 does refer specifically to the messianic kingdom, but the people probably have in mind the popular political hope. Perhaps Jesus chose this mode of entry to reveal the nature of his messiahship to those prepared to see it, and to conceal it from the rest.

We are in the midst of a scene of considerable tension. The crowd seems aware of some sort of impending crisis; the disciples are bewildered but following along; the authorities are prepared to strike at any moment; and in the midst of it all is a solitary, determined, and no doubt sorrowful, figure determined to press through to the end.

Verse 11 makes ready for the cleansing of the temple. Jesus apparently stays at Bethany from Sunday to Wednesday of the last week.

b. the cursing of the fig tree, 11:12-14

This is a difficult story, not merely because it is a nature miracle, but because of the rather petulant picture it draws of Jesus, withering a tree because it was not bearing fruit several months before its normal time. Probably the best explanation is that originally this was in the form of a parable, describing Israel as a withered tree that no longer bears fruit (see Luke 13: 6-9). But in the process of oral transmission it became transformed into a narrative of an actual historical event. Mark puts the story here, in any case, to point to the coming events as decisive proof of the barrenness of the old Israel.

c. the cleansing of the temple, 11:15-19

Jesus now enters into the forecourt of the temple (sometimes called the court of the Gentiles, for it was the only place the non-Jew was allowed to pray). He drove out the officials who sold purified birds for animal sacrifices and the money-changers who exchanged (at a good profit for the priests) the popular Roman money for the Jewish coin which alone could be used for the temple dues. The action is more than that of a religious reformer protesting against corruption. It is also an act of messianic symbolism for those able to understand. In Malachi 3:1 we read: ". . . the Lord whom you seek will suddenly come to his temple; the messenger of the covenant in whom you delight, behold, he is coming, says the Lord of hosts." So here the cleansing is a symbol of the coming of God's new covenant in the person of his chosen Messiah. Notice that Jesus does not hesitate to use force to accomplish his purpose. How does this action fit in with Jesus' words about nonresistance to evil in Matthew 5:39 and love of enemies in Matthew 5:43-44?

d. the fig tree—results; and sayings on prayer and faith, 11:20-25

Verses 20-21 present the conclusion to the fig-tree incident. To this, Mark has attached a loose collection of Jesus' sayings. The context is unfortunate. Doubtless Jesus had often spoken of faith in God, but as a response to the cursing and withering of the tree, the saying in verses 22-23 takes on a trivial flavor. Of course, verse 23 is not meant to be taken literally. This is simply a way of saying that with faith in God men can perform what seems impossible. Verse 25 reflects a knowledge of the Sermon on the Mount (Matthew 6:14) and suggests that it was known in some form in Rome in the 70's.

2. teaching in Jerusalem, 11:27—13:37

a. a series of questions from the Pharisees and others, 11:27—12:34

The apparent purpose of this series of questions was to trap Jesus into a premature and public avowal of his messiahship, and thus into an act of blasphemy for which he could be arrested.

1. *what is your authority?*, 11:27-33

The priests, the teachers, and the high-ranking members of the Sanhedrin or ruling court confront Jesus. Their question is a menacing one, not for information. Jesus replies by asking another question, about John the Baptist. Was God with John or not? If they said no, the people who liked John would be offended. If they said yes, they'd have to admit that God was inspiring Jesus as well.

2. *parenthetical story of the wicked tenants*, 12:1-12

This can be read both as a forthright advance accusation against the Pharisees as murderers (12:7-8), and also as a prediction of the rejection by God of the Jews (verses 9-10). The story becomes vivid when we make a few identifications in the allegory:

the vineyard is Israel; the owner is God; the tenants are the Jews; the servants are the prophets and perhaps John the Baptist; the son is Christ.

3. *may God's people pay tribute to a worldly state? 12:13-17*

This incident refers to a poll tax which all Jews under Roman occupation had to pay. After the somewhat obvious flattery of verse 14, they put the question to him. It was probably a burning question, for some of the extreme Jewish nationalists were against the tax, though the Pharisees on the whole supported it. A "no" would have given the Jews a chance to portray Jesus to the Romans as seditious; a clear "yes" would have had a bad popular effect on the ordinary man. Jesus' answer refers to this particular issue, and cannot be taken as a general guide to all the problems of political responsibility. Jesus was no revolutionary; the tax was only twenty cents a year; the coin is Caesar's anyway—why not let him have it! Other situations might arise when giving Caesar what is his might compromise allegiance to God, but this is not one of them. In such cases, "We must obey God rather than men" (Acts 5:29) would represent a part of the truth that needed stressing. A good political ethic should have both Jesus' word here, and the word from Acts.

4. do the dead rise?, 12:12-27

The Sadducees were priestly aristocrats, quite conversative, rejecting many of the theological innovations, like belief in the resurrection of the body, which the Pharisees affirmed. To understand the challenge here, we should refer to Deuteronomy 25:5 where the law of levirate marriage is set down: if a man dies without children, his brother must marry the widow. The Sadducees take an extreme case to challenge Jesus' belief in the resurrection.

Jesus responds with a double accusation. The Sadducees are ignorant of the scriptures (a telling blow, since they based their denial of the resurrection on the silence of the Torah, the first five Old Testament books), and they do not trust the power of God. Verse 25 indicates that the future life is a different order of existence from the present. "Like angels" simply means in perfect communion with God. He quotes, to make his case, from that part of the Old Testament which the Sadducees took as authoritative, in this case Exodus 3:6. If God is rightly called the God of the living, and if he is also the God of Abraham, Isaac, and Jacob, then these patriarchs must be said to be living with God.

This is a rather polemical answer, but it is effective. Its real significance lies in the fact that Jesus bases the hope for immortality not on something inherent or immortal in man, but on the power and grace of God.

5. *what is the chief commandment?*, 12:28-34

Here the questioner seems friendly, genuinely asking for information. When we recall that the rabbis distinguished 613 different commandments in the law, we can understand why an earnest Jew might ask such a question.

Jesus responds by citing two separate Old Testament passages, Deuteronomy 6:4 and Leviticus 19:18, which had not before been put together in this way. Verses 29-30 are from the Shema, the prayer which every pious Jew repeated daily. The enumeration of the various faculties merely stresses the total claim of God on man.

"As yourself," in verse 31, has always given trouble. Is this really a third commandment to love the self? Or is Jesus taking our extreme but misdirected self-love as an example of the intensity of love which ought to be directed to the neighbor? Is he saying:

Love your neighbor with all the concern and passion with which, as a sinner, you now love yourself?

b. the Messiah is not David's son, 12:35-37

When we remember that the Son of David type of messianic thinking had a strongly political and nationalistic flavor, we can see why Jesus rejects certain ways of thinking about the Davidic descent of the Messiah.

c. against the scribes, 12:37-40

Having rejected some of the scribes' teaching, having just praised a sympathetic scribe's response, Jesus here turns to a criticism of their religious practice, making a devastating attack on religious professionalism. "Devouring widows' houses" probably refers to some form of financial gain based on spiritual influence over pious women, perhaps involving persuasion of the ladies to turn over their property to the clergy.

d. the widow's offering, 12:41-44

Jesus knows how much money is put in the box not because he had supernatural knowledge but probably because the amount of the gift was called out by the priests.

e. the apocalyptic discourse, 13:1-37

Most observers agree today that this chapter is a composite one, containing some general apocalyptic material from Mark's own time, as well as some genuine reflections of Jesus' own teaching. But just what does apocalyptic mean? It is a particular way of thinking about the present and the future, and it can be contrasted with the prophetic type of thought. The prophet knew that God was acting here and now, in the present events of history, and he occasionally spoke of God's action in the immediate future. Apocalyptic, we might say, is prophecy become radically pessimistic. When the present state of history and culture looks unusually black, God's immediate action in it is not so clearly seen, and the apocalyptic thinker looks far into the future, finding his hope and resting place there. His pessimism is so acute that he feels God can act only by means of some cosmic catastrophe and, instead of describing God's action now, he describes the details of that future catastrophe. Even if God does not seem to be in control now, the apocalyptist in effect says, in the final days He will be Lord of all things. We might say that the current fascination that science fiction has for some people lies just at this point: frustrated with politics and with the problem of the immediate future, man may turn to the catastrophe of the end, and speculate about what will happen then. If politics is secular prophecy, science fiction may well be called secular apocalyptic.

Let us turn to this elusive Chapter 13. The early church historian Eusebius mentions in his writings an "oracle" that warned Christians in Jerusalem to flee at the start of the Roman siege of that city in A.D. 70, and verses 6-8, 14-20, 24-27, could very well be part of that oracle rather than words of Jesus.

The whole chapter falls into the following divisions:

(1) Jesus' prediction of the destruction of the temple, verses 1-2

This was Herod's temple, begun in 20 B.C., and said to be a beautiful building. It was destroyed in A.D. 70.

(2) introduction to the discourse, verses 3-4

The disciples question Jesus about his prediction, and his response is the discourse proper. But instead of speaking of the fall of the temple, Jesus gives a detailed account of the events leading up to the end of the world.

(3) the first stage of the drama, verses
    5-13

First, false messiahs will appear, claiming
man's allegiance. Then will follow war,
earthquakes, famines. This order of events
is quite common in both Jewish and Christian apocalyptic writing of this kind. The
sayings here have always been fertile
ground for Christian groups predicting
the end of the world after every historical
catastrophe.

(4) the second stage, verses 14-23

An act of outrage to the temple is described.
The "desolating sacrilege," of verse 14,
refers to Daniel 9:27 and 11:31 where the
pagan pollution of the temple by Antiochus
Epiphanes is described. It is not clear here
just what sort of act is being predicted,
perhaps some sort of violence done by one
of the expected false messiahs.

Observe that verses 15-18 can very

easily be understood as words of warning to Christians in Jerusalem under Roman attack, rather than as warnings about the end of the world. There is some reflection of Daniel 12 here.

(5) the final stage, verses 24-27

Here the climax, a cosmic catastrophe followed by the coming of the Son of man, is described. This section is composed almost entirely of Old Testament quotation and paraphrase, and is too unoriginal to be taken as exact words of Jesus.

(6) conclusion to the chapter: on watchfulness, verses 28-37

Placed here at the end of this chapter, these warnings are made to speak of watchfulness in the face of the coming Son of man. Verse 28, however, could originally have been a saying of Jesus preparing the disciples for the crisis of his own ministry. Verse 32, suggesting that not even Jesus himself knows the time of the final consummation, must be genuine, as the early church would hardly have invented this admission of ignorance. The little parable in verses 34-36 may originally have been a word of Jesus preparing his disciples for the interval between his death and resurrection.

Thus, this chapter seems to contain some general apocalyptic material that was possibly used by the church in preparation for the destruction of Jerusalem, as well as some authentic sayings of Jesus, uttered in one context, but placed by Mark in the setting of the final consummation. The chapter as a whole presents many difficulties, but, in an age when persecution and catastrophe are not unknown to the church, it is not irrelevant; and the whole of it speaks movingly of the power of God and of his concern for his people even in the worst of times.

VI. The Passion and Resurrection Narratives
14:1—16:8 (9-20)

THIS FINAL SECTION is the most coherent and flowing in the whole of Mark's gospel, and this material was probably the first to be committed to writing. Only by such a detailed narrative could the pressing questions be answered: How did Jesus die, and why?

1. events leading up to the arrest, 14:1-52

a. the plot, 14:1-2

It is now Wednesday of holy week, and the priests and scribes decide to take Jesus at once, and privately, in view of the crowds gathering for the passover celebration. Jesus had many sympathizers, and a public arrest might cause an uprising.

b. the anointing at Bethany, 14:3-9

This strange story has two difficulties. First, what is the meaning of "For you always have the poor with you" in verse 7? This verse, taken out of context, has been put to irresponsible use in the history of Christianity, as if it were a divine sanction on poverty and a discouragement to all attempts to fight against it. The saying here must be understood as part of Jesus' commendation of the uniqueness of the woman's act. You are always commissioned to serve the poor, Jesus is saying. But this woman's act expresses a unique insight into my ministry and God's purpose, and therefore it is a worthy and beautiful thing. Second, what was there in the act that merited such praise from Jesus? Two things: the jar was broken, and Jesus was anointed. The word "Messiah" means "anointed one," and so the woman is confessing Jesus as the Messiah or Christ. But the breaking of the jar suggests that she

knows the deeper meaning of his messiahship, that suffering and death await him. The
disciples had not yet come up to this level.

c. Judas' betrayal, 14:10-11

What did Judas betray and why? These two
questions have been the subject of endless
debate. Perhaps he told the priests of Jesus'
messianic claims; more likely (as is hinted
here) he told them where and how they
could find Jesus so that he could be arrested
without a public commotion. (See John
11:57.)

But why? Whether he did it for the money,
or to force Jesus into a situation where he
could display his divine power and so bring
in the kingdom by force, or out of personal
disappointment at the apparent failure of
the mission, or because he was evil from the
beginning (but then why did Jesus call him
in the first place?)—we simply do not know.
(See John 13:2.)

d. preparing for the Passover, 14:12-16

It is now the next day, Thursday, and the disciples ask about preparations for the Passover meal that evening. Jesus' answer indicates that he has already made arrangements with some friend in the city, and he directs two of the disciples to the place.

e. the betrayal predicted, 14:17-21

Jesus has discerned the character of Judas, and announces the betrayal without pointing him out. Verse 21 indicates the divine necessity of the death, but also serves as a solemn warning to Judas.

f. the last supper, 14:22-25

In I Corinthians 11:23-26, we have an independent account of this incident which is remarkably similar. Only Paul mentions the commandment to repeat the rite, though (since Paul's letter is some years earlier than

Mark's gospel) by Mark's time it has doubtless become so customary that it didn't need to be mentioned. The words over the bread and the wine differ slightly.

In reading this, recall three facts. (1) Jesus had compared the kingdom of God to a banquet (Luke 14:15-24), and this meal can be seen as a foretaste or a rehearsal of the full messianic banquet in heaven at the end of time (verse 25 here hints at this, too). (2) The Passover, which Mark relates to this supper (the trial and death take place on Passover in Mark, though not in John), commemorated the election by God of Israel as his special people, but Jesus had already made clear that the Jews were forfeiting this status in rejecting the Messiah. A new people is being formed; a new covenant, a new election, is being offered by God. (3) Jesus had already spoken of giving his life for "many" (Mark 10:45), and had described his suffering as a "cup" (Mark 10:38, and see also 14:36).

So this rite portrays the new life of the kingdom of God, pointing forward to the death and resurrection. He is doing here symbolically what he was to do the next day in fact. Standing before them, breaking the bread, he says, "This means my body." Pouring and distributing the wine, he says, "This means my life (the blood is the source of life in Hebrew thought), given to you."

The actions of breaking and pouring, therefore, are just as important as the words Jesus speaks. And when Christians, in many different ways, gather together to celebrate the sacrament of the Lord's Supper, Holy Communion, Eucharist, or Mass, the words and gestures together form the total meaning. We, like the disciples in the upper room, need something more than mere words about God and Christ. We need gestures to see; tangible things, like bread and wine, to touch and taste. This is one of the meanings of the Christian sacraments.

g. prediction of Peter's denial, 14:26-31

After the traditional passover hymn (part of Psalms 115-118), the little group leaves the upper room and goes out to the evening camp. Jesus has been reflecting on the effect his death will have on the disciples, and he tells them they will all flee away. He is shortly proved correct. Verse 28 indicates that only after the resurrection will they be reassembled. Impetuous Peter protests his loyalty, and his denial is predicted. (As an example of the kind of interesting detail you can discover if you turn to the commentaries, note that the "cock crow" is the name of the Roman trumpet call announcing the beginning of the fourth watch at 3:00 A.M.)

h. Gethsemane, 14:32-42

This scene needs little comment. Even at this late hour, Jesus asks that his time of suffering ("the hour") might pass by, that he not have to drink the cup of suffering, death, and even judgment (15:34 suggests something of what this "cup" really involves). After this bold request (there is no premature acquiescence in Jesus' prayer), he submits his will to God's. And the disciples sleep through it all.

i. arrest, 14:43-52

The priests, along with a hired gang led by Judas, appear. Judas identifies his master with the traditional kiss of the pupil for his teacher.

The little picture in verses 51-52 is odd. Some have thought that Mark is describing himself here; some consider that it is a detail suggested by Amos 2:16; others simply say it is a genuine, if irrelevant historical detail— genuine, for there seems to be no reason why the early church would have made it up.

2. the trial, crucifixion, and burial, 14:53— 15:47

a. the trial before the high priests, 14:53-65

The trial of Jesus is in two parts: the ecclesiastical trial before Caiaphas and the civil trial before Pilate.

It is midnight now, and a group is hastily assembled to hear the evidence. Witnesses can't seem to agree—not even on the supposed prediction of the destruction of the temple. Jesus answers the high priest, declaring himself to be the Messiah and Son of God. The quotation from Daniel 7:13 in verse 62 is not a statement about the second coming, but about Jesus' ascension to God with power.

Verse 63 presents the priest responding in the prescribed way to an act of blasphemy. The charge is blasphemy, but the Jewish courts probably do not have the power of capital punishment (see John 18:31).

b. Peter's denial, 14:66-72

The vivid details here suggest that this story is a reminiscence of Peter. He moves from the courtyard to the front porch of the high priest's palace to avoid the girl's questions, but she talks to some of the bystanders who apparently recognize Peter's Galilean accent.

c. the ecclesiastical trial is ratified, 15:1

Meetings of the Sanhedrin after sunset being unofficial (14:53-65), they assemble again in the morning (Friday) to confirm the charge of blasphemy. Since they apparently cannot put him to death, they take Jesus off to Pilate, hoping to establish a charge of treason from his claim to be king of the Jews, and so to convince the governor that he is dangerous to law and order.

d. the civil trial before Pilate, 15:2-15

Pilate's first question indicates that the priests have been stressing the political aspects of Jesus' guilt. The answer in verse 2 is probably a "yes," but with the implication: "That is not my way of putting it, for I have no political or nationalistic pretensions." In any case, Pilate remains unconvinced by Jewish charges (verses 5, 10). Perhaps he was inclined at first to release Jesus, and certainly he considered him harmless. But the priests have brought a mob of supporters into the courtyard, and they are pressing for the release of Barabbas and the conviction of Jesus. Pilate is reluctant, but he is unwilling to risk a disturbance and is anxious for his popular reputation, so he finally gives in.

The relative guilt of Roman and Jew in all this has been much discussed. Certainly Mark lays the blame pretty heavily on the

Jews, and is almost sympathetic to the weak and vacillating Pilate. And the other gospels give even more sympathetic accounts of the Roman judge. Perhaps Mark is interested in suggesting to whatever Roman officials who might read his gospel that the Roman power was relatively guiltless in the affair. But doubtless both groups, along with the crowd itself, are equally implicated.

e. the soldiers mock Jesus, 15:16-20

The soldiers' barracks were in Herod's palace, and here they bring Jesus.

f. crucifixion and death, 15:21-41

In Roman crucifixion, which was the penalty for slaves, the victim was compelled to carry the crossbar to the site. Then, his outstretched arms were tied or nailed to the crossbar, the crossbar attached to the upright, the feet fixed to the upright, and the cross then set in the ground and raised aloft.

Death ordinarily was slow, taking as long as two or three days, and was usually caused by exposure.

Golgotha was apparently a skull-shaped hill outside the city, but its location cannot be identified today. Simon is chosen from the crowd to carry the piece when Jesus falters. The mention of Simon's sons suggests that they were known to Mark and to the church at Rome (see Romans 16:13).

Jesus refuses the drug, wishing to die with an unclouded mind (and remember 14:25). His clothing becomes the property of the executioners, and the soldiers throw dice for it (see Psalm 22:18). He is crucified—that is, nailed to the cross—at 9:00 A.M. The superscription, giving the offense, was on a chalked board over his head. The charge as written shows that Jesus was officially executed by the Romans, and on the charge of claiming to be king—of course a distortion of the true messiahship as Mark and Jesus himself understood it.

As he hung there, some of the crowd, the chief priests, and even the robbers on either side joined in the general mockery. Of course, the Jewish taunt is true: he did save others, and he did not save himself, for his whole conception of the suffering Messiah meant that in order for others to be saved, he must not consider his own fate.

From noon until 3:00 P.M., it grew dark. This may be a symbolic touch, related to the portents often associated in the ancient world with the death of heroes (see *Julius Caesar,* Act 1, scene 3), or it may refer to an actual dust storm to which Mark gives a deeper significance. At 3:00 P.M., the terrible cry from Psalm 22:1 is uttered. Mark gives the Aramaic version, and translates it for his readers. This cry presents a problem too deep to be fully understood, but we can begin to grasp it if we find here a genuine, if temporary, feeling of desolation and separation from God. For Christians it is a pointer to the reality and the cost of Jesus' bearing the sin of the world, and even to the cost to God of his gift of salvation. The onlookers misunderstand, and think Jesus is calling for Elijah. At 3:00 P.M., after a cry of victory, he dies.

The curtain of the temple is torn (verse 38)—either a symbol of the destruction of Jewish religion and the temple itself, or of the breakdown of the barriers between the presence of God and men. The curtain mentioned served in the temple to shut off the Holy of Holies (where God was supposed to be specially present) from the sight of the congregation. Only the priest could ever enter the place. This curtain is torn at the moment of death.

The centurion heard the final cry of victory, and is impressed by the manner of Jesus' death. His remark, though not a full Christian confession, is at least a mark of admiration. Verses 40-41 serve as a transition to the burial and resurrection stories, and also they may suggest Mark's sources for the crucifixion story itself.

g. *burial, 15:42-47*

It was against Jewish law to leave bodies hanging overnight, and especially on a Sabbath. (It was now perhaps 4:00 P.M., just a few hours before sunset and the beginning of the Sabbath and Passover.) Joseph, a member of the Sanhedrin (probably in Arimathea, not the Jerusalem group that tried Jesus), asks Pilate for the body.

The close of the story seems to be unrelieved tragedy. No disciple is present; only a few sympathetic women look on from a distance; the last acts of piety are performed by a respectable Jew who probably never knew Jesus.

3. *the resurrection, 16:1-8*

Saturday at sunset, when the Sabbath is officially over, the women collect spices to anoint the body in the tomb. (Matthew and John say that the women merely go to see the body; Mark and Luke, that they go to anoint it.) Early the following morning they go to the tomb. They find the large stone rolled away and a young man (explicitly called an angel in Matthew 28:2-5, but only indirectly here) tells them that Jesus has risen from the grave. They hear that he is to appear in Galilee; and they rush out of the tomb in astonishment and fear. Mark makes no attempt to say how the stone was moved; doubtless he thought it was the work of God or of the risen Christ.

With the words in verse 8, "for they were afraid," the true text of Mark comes to an end. The Revised Standard Version includes, in the footnotes, both a longer ending (which appears in the King James version as part of the text) and a shorter ending which appears in some manuscripts. But it is agreed that neither of these endings is Mark's. Some feel that the ending (with verse

8) as it stands is what Mark intended, that it is effective and dramatic; some feel that the original ending has been lost, either because Mark was interrupted in his composition (the persecutions?) or because the manuscript became torn off at the end.

When one compares the five different accounts we have of the resurrection (this, Matthew 28:1-10, Luke 24:1-11, John 20:1-10, and I Corinthians 15:3-7) there are a number of details that are impossible to harmonize. Mark may have allowed himself some imaginative freedom in depicting the scene—the story of the young man, for instance. What can hardly be called legendary or imaginative, however, is the double fact that the tomb was empty and that Jesus appeared to his followers after his death.

How can we interpret the fact of the empty tomb? If we say that the Jews or Romans stole the body, it would have been simple for them to put a stop to the preaching of the resurrection simply by producing

it, but this they did not do. If we say that
the disciples stole and hid the body, we have
a picture of the whole origin of the Christian
movement based on a piece of crude decep-
tion. Even Jewish commentators on this material find this hypothesis incredible.

Our remaining alternative is to say that
God in fact did raise Jesus from the dead,
changing his "physical body" into a "spiritual
body," and in this latter form he appeared to
his followers.

The transformation of the dispirited and
cowardly disciples into forthright evangelists,
the very existence of the church and the New
Testament—these facts receive an adequate
explanation only when we go beyond the
general statement, "Jesus conquered death,"
to the explicit and factual remark that *God
raised Jesus Christ from the dead.* This is
scarcely an easy statement for any of us to
make, for we are all modern men. And yet—
though there is room for openness and even
agnosticism on some of the details of the

resurrection narrative—it seems certain that no qualification can be accepted of the actual, historical fact of the resurrection as a decisive and mighty act of God for man's salvation and eternal life.